Knock knock JOKES

By **Ima Laffin**

BIG BUDDY

JOKES

Big Buddy Books
An imprint of Abdo Publishing
abdopublishing.com

abdopublishing.com

Published by Abdo Publishing, a division of ABDO, PO Box 398166, Minneapolis, Minnesota 55439.
Copyright © 2017 by Abdo Consulting Group, Inc. International copyrights reserved in all countries.
No part of this book may be reproduced in any form without written permission from the publisher.
Big Buddy Books™ is a trademark and logo of Abdo Publishing.

Printed in the United States of America, North Mankato, Minnesota.
082016
012017

 THIS BOOK CONTAINS
RECYCLED MATERIALS

Illustrations: Sunny Grey/Spectrum Studio

Coordinating Series Editor: Tamara L. Britton
Contributing Editor: Katie Lajiness
Graphic Design: Taylor Higgins

Publisher's Cataloging-in-Publication Data

Names: Laffin, Ima, author.
Title: Knock-knock jokes / by Ima Laffin.
Description: Minneapolis, MN : Abdo Publishing, 2017. | Series: Big buddy jokes
Identifiers: LCCN 2016944868 | ISBN 9781680785128 (lib. bdg.) | ISBN
    9781680798722 (ebook)
Subjects: LCSH: Knock-knock jokes--Juvenile humor. | Wit and humor--Juvenile
    humor.
Classification: DDC 818/.602--dc23
LC record available at http://lccn.loc.gov/2016944868

Knock knock!

Who's there?

Boo.

Boo who?

Don't cry! It's only a joke.

Knock knock!

Who's there?

Cargo.

Cargo who?

Car go beep beep.

Knock knock!

Who's there?

Pizza.

Pizza who?

Pizza really great guy!

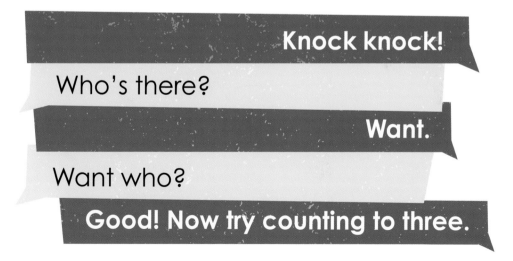

Knock knock!

Who's there?

Want.

Want who?

Good! Now try counting to three.

Knock knock!

Who's there?

Water.

Water who?

Water we waiting for?

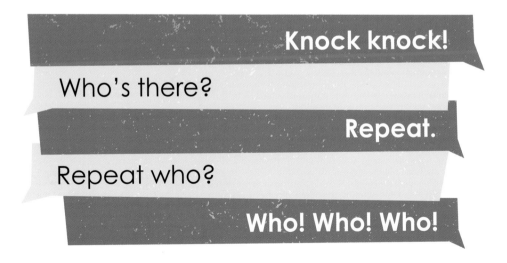

Knock knock!

Who's there?

Repeat.

Repeat who?

Who! Who! Who!

Knock knock!

Who's there?

Dishwasher.

Dishwasher who?

Dishwasher way I spoke before I had false teeth!

Knock knock!

Who's there?

Gorilla.

Gorilla who?

Gorilla me a sandwich please.

Knock knock!

Who's there?

Amy!

Amy who?

Amy fraid I've forgotten!

Knock knock!

Who's there?

Abby!

Abby who?

Abby stung me on the nose!

Knock knock!

Who's there?

Dot.

Dot who?

Dot's for me to know, and you to find out.

Knock knock!

Who's there?

Anita!

Anita who?

Anita borrow a pencil!

Knock knock!

Who's there?

Isabel.

Isabel who?

Isabel necessary on a bicycle?

Knock knock!

Who's there?

Ketchup.

Ketchup who?

Ketchup to me and I will tell you.

Knock knock!

Who's there?

Philip.

Philip who?

Philip my glass please!

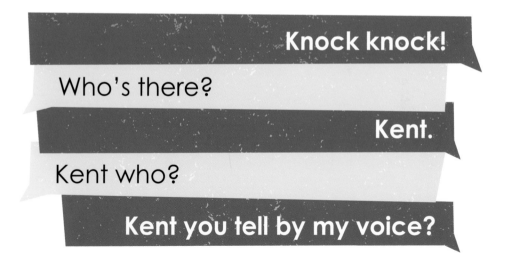

Knock knock!

Who's there?

Kent.

Kent who?

Kent you tell by my voice?

Knock knock!

Who's there?

Barb.

Barb who?

Barbecue.

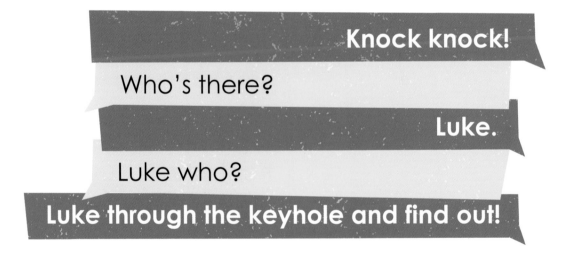

Knock knock!

Who's there?

Luke.

Luke who?

Luke through the keyhole and find out!

15

Knock knock!

Who's there?

Oink oink.

Oink oink who?

Make up your mind if you're going to be a pig or an owl!

Knock knock!

Who's there?

Ice cream.

Ice cream who?

Ice cream if you throw me in cold water!

Will you remember me in an hour?

Sure.

Will you remember me in a minute?

Sure.

Will you remember me in a second?

Sure.

Knock knock!

Who's there?

You forgot me already!

Knock knock!

Who's there?

Amos.

Amos who?

A mosquito bit me.

Knock knock!

Who's there?

A little girl.

A little girl who?

A little girl who can't reach the doorbell.

Knock knock!

Who's there?

Olive.

Olive who?

Olive my mom!

Knock knock!

Who's there?

Who.

Who who?

You don't who, owls do!

Knock knock!

Who's there?

Doris.

Doris who?

Doris open, come on in.

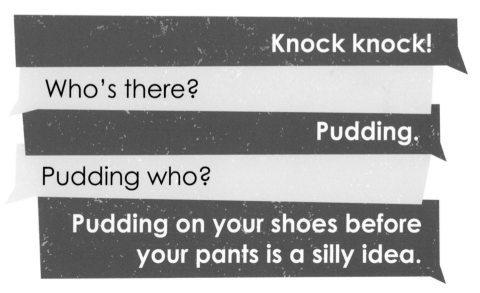

Knock knock!

Who's there?

Pudding.

Pudding who?

Pudding on your shoes before your pants is a silly idea.

Knock knock!

Who's there?

Tuba.

Tuba who?

Tuba toothpaste!

Knock knock!

Who's there?

Yah!

Yah who?

Did I just hear a cowboy?

Knock knock!

Who's there?

Peas.

Peas who?

Peas to meet you!

Knock knock!

Who's there?

Little old lady.

Little old lady who?

I didn't know you could yodel!

Knock knock!

Who's there?

Cook.

Cook who?

Stop making bird noises and open the door!

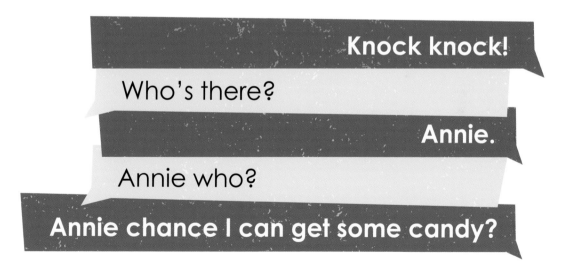

Knock knock!

Who's there?

Annie.

Annie who?

Annie chance I can get some candy?

Knock knock!

Who's there?

Cows.

Cows who?

Cows go "moo" not "who"!

Knock knock!

Who's there?

Howard.

Howard who?

Howard I know?

26

Knock knock!

Who's there?

Pig.

Pig who?

Pig up your feet or you'll trip!

27

Knock knock!

Who's there?

Tank.

Tank who?

You're welcome!

Knock knock!

Who's there?

Wire.

Wire who?

Wire you asking?

Knock knock!

Who's there?

Duey.

Duey who?

Duey have to keep telling knock knock jokes?

Knock knock!

Who's there?

Police.

Police who?

Police stop telling these awful knock knock jokes.

Knock knock!

Who's there?

Candace.

Candace who?

Candace be the last knock knock joke?

Knock knock!

Who's there?

Lettuce.

Lettuce who?

Lettuce in and I'll tell ya!

31

WEBSITES

To learn more about Big Buddy Jokes, visit **booklinks.abdopublishing.com**. These links are routinely monitored and updated to provide the most current information available.